KEYBOARD *Signature Licks*

Best
Bebop Piano

by
Gene Rizzo

CONTENTS

In Memoriam
Earl "Bud" Powell • 1924 - 1966
Sui Generis et Vox Dei

Cover Photo by Peter Amft

ISBN 0-634-02690-9

HAL•LEONARD®
CORPORATION
7777 W. BLUEMOUND RD. P.O. BOX 13819 MILWAUKEE, WI 53213

Visit Hal Leonard Online at
www.halleonard.com

INTRODUCTION

Bebop dominated the jazz scene from the mid-forties to the end of the decade and beyond. There were isolated pre-war rumblings of this unique genre, but basically its parameters were set by a handful of like-minded rebels in jam sessions at two New York City nightclubs: Minton's Playhouse and Monroe's Uptown.

Boppers substantially redefined the swing style of the thirties. Chordal extensions (9ths, 11ths, and 13ths), formerly the domain of modern classical music, were recruited from the scores of Debussy, Ravel, and Stravinsky. Melody, enriched by chromatic voice-leading, was liberated from the almost exclusive use of chord tones. The monotony of equal quarter-note stress in common time was relieved by freely emphasizing the second and fourth beats.

Such a revolution in music called for fresh technical approaches on all instruments; the piano was no exception. The modified stride of Art Tatum and other swing pianists no longer served the needs of harnessing the raw materials of bebop. A new paradigm emerged: Bud Powell.

Already a virtuoso in his mid-teens, Powell's frequent participation in the jam sessions at Minton's exposed him to the high priests of the movement. Inspired by the fluid horn lines of Charlie Parker and Dizzy Gillespie and the benefit of a deep, abiding friendship with the house pianist, Thelonious Monk, Powell forged an influential synthesis of these elements, adding important innovations of his own as well.

Powell and his many disciples took center stage in the jazz piano community. If improvisational skill is the quintessence of jazz playing, these pianists (many of whom are surveyed in this book) have raised the bar more than a few notches. Studying a period of such rampant creativity can only be rewarding.

Gene Rizzo

DISCOGRAPHY

The performances transcribed in this volume can be found on the following CDs and/or records:

SATIN DOLL - *Red Garland at the Prelude, Vol. 1*
        Prestige PRCD-24132

IF I WERE A BELL - *Relaxin' with the Miles Davis Quintet*
        Prestige OJCCD-190

EAST OF THE SUN (AND WEST OF THE MOON) - *Charlie Parker—The Complete Live Performances on Savoy*
        Savoy Jazz SVY-17021

BODY AND SOUL - *Listen to Barry Harris*
        Riverside OJCCD-999

I REMEMBER YOU - *Everybody Likes Hampton Hawes, Vol. 3 The Trio*
        Contemporary OJCCD-421

AS LONG AS I LIVE - Hank Jones—*"Hanky Panky"*
        Inner City IC6020

THINGS AIN'T WHAT THEY USED TO BE - Hank Jones—*Blusette*
        Black & Blue 33168

ON A CLEAR DAY (YOU CAN SEE FOREVER) - The Wynton Kelly Trio—*Full View*
        Milestone OJCCD-912

APRIL IN PARIS - *Thelonious Himself*
        Riverside OJCCD-254

BETWEEN THE DEVIL AND THE DEEP BLUE SEA - *Monk Alone—The Complete Solo Studio Recordings 1962–1968*
        Columbia C2K65495

CHEROKEE, HALLUCINATIONS - *The Complete Bud Powell on Verve*
        Verve 314-521-669

LULLABY OF BIRDLAND - *The Best of George Shearing*
        Capitol 72435-20157

THOU SWELL, PRELUDE TO A KISS - *Horace Silver Trio*
        Blue Note CDP7-81520

I DON'T STAND A GHOST OF A CHANCE - *Lennie Tristano Supersonic*
        Definitive DRCD-11132

WILLIAM "RED" GARLAND
1923–1984

Dallas-born, Garland flirted with the clarinet and the alto saxophone in his teens. His more serious aspirations as a professional boxer were sidetracked by the draft. While serving in the Army, he took up the piano at the non-prodigy age of twenty. Discharged in 1944, he was already holding his own as pianist in a group led by "Hot Lips" Page. In 1946, he joined the Billy Eckstine big band, which featured several key members of the emerging bebop school, an experience that had a lasting impact on his style.

Gigs with Coleman Hawkins, Roy Eldridge, and the other icons followed, but it was his long stint with Miles Davis's quintet (1955 to 1959) that brought him fame. Garland, bassist Paul Chambers, and drummer Philly Joe Jones were known as *the* rhythm section of the fifties and provided hair-trigger time for Miles and John Coltrane in that historic group.

Leaving Miles in 1959, Garland recorded extensively, mostly leading trios. He returned to his native Dallas upon the death of his mother in 1965 and remained there. Except for occasional recording dates in New York, he retired from the scene. It is said that he did not own a piano at the time of his death.

To Garland's credit as an artist, he never indulged in the "Bud Powell lite" style that so many pianists of his generation played. Although Powell was an important influence, Garland tempered it with the less percussive, elegant touch of Nat Cole.

IF I WERE A BELL
from *GUYS AND DOLLS*
By Frank Loesser

Figure 1–Solo Break and First 16 Measures

Garland's solo is a cheerful antidote to the angst in the John Coltrane solo that precedes it. The solo break (measures 1–2) sets up the II chord (G13 in measure 3) by way of its dominant (D7#9), laced with extensions and alterations. Garland's four-measure phrases avoid the steady stream of eighth notes so characteristic of typical bebop pianists. Triplets and sixteenths vary the lines, as well as a judicious use of space.

Fig. 1

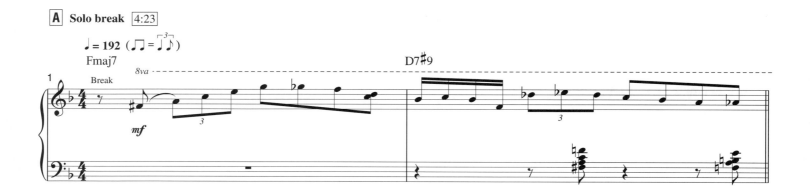

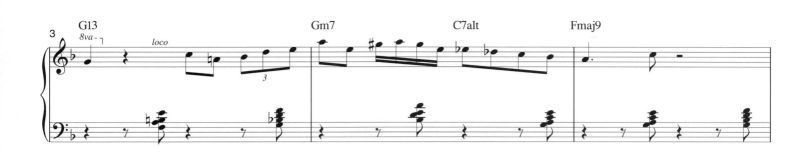

Figure 2–Solo (Last 4 Measures Extended by Turnarounds)

    Tag endings for solos were the Miles Davis Quintet of the fifties stock-in-trade. Garland romps through II–V–III–VI turnarounds, generally reserving chord tones for downbeats and passing tones for upbeats. The two blues licks ending on A♭ (measures 16–19) deliberately do not agree with their accompanying chords. Measures 20–23 are typical Garland block chord voicings: a melody above middle C stated in octaves, divided by 5ths and supported by three- or four-note chords in the tenor register of the piano. The bell tone in the last measure is a sly nod to the song's title.

Fig. 2

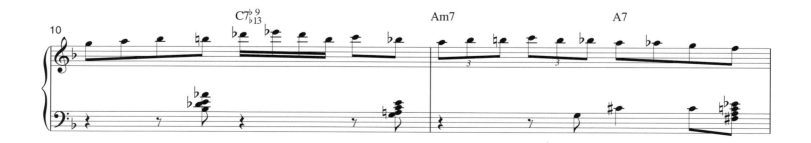

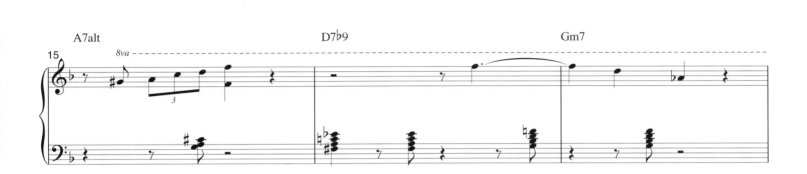

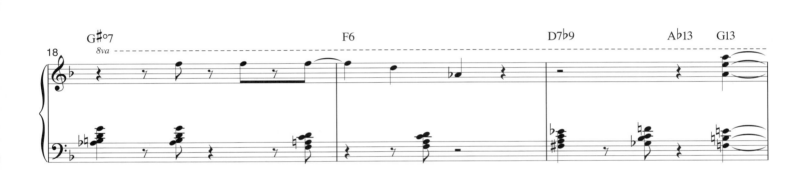

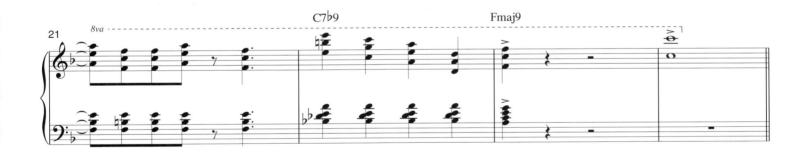

SATIN DOLL
from *SOPHISTICATED LADIES*
By Duke Ellington

Figure 3–Head (First 8 Measures)

Garland uses his block chord style for this jazz classic and chooses to play it in B♭ instead of the original key, C. His left-hand chords are rootless; the anchors are left to the bass player. These chords gently push the beat along on upbeats. The glissando in measure 5 is appropriately sassy for this tune and treatment.

Fig. 3

Figure 4–Head (Bridge)

We find more block chords here, but Garland reharmonizes measures 1 and 2, avoiding the conventional II–V sequence (Fm7 to B♭7) with dominant chords (F7 and C♭9).

Fig. 4

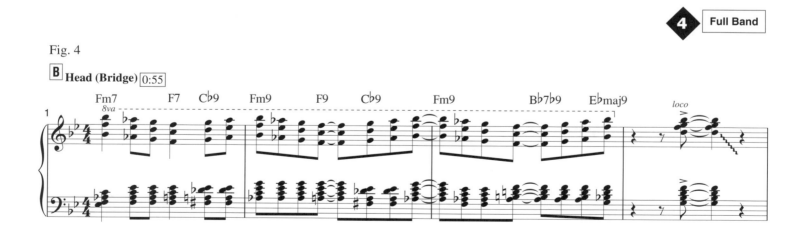

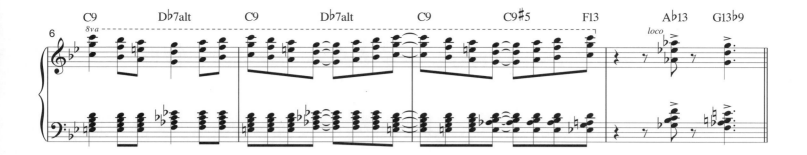

Figure 5–Solo (Bridge)

The grace notes (measure 4) and the riff that highlights the #11 (F# in measures 5–7) are typical of this pianist's good-natured playing.

Fig. 5

Figure 6–Solo (Last 8 Measures)

Garland's glissandos persist through measures 4–7. Inspired by Nat Cole, one of Garland's influences, they occur on upbeats to achieve maximum impact and drive. They are always spearheaded by a dissonant non-chordal note.

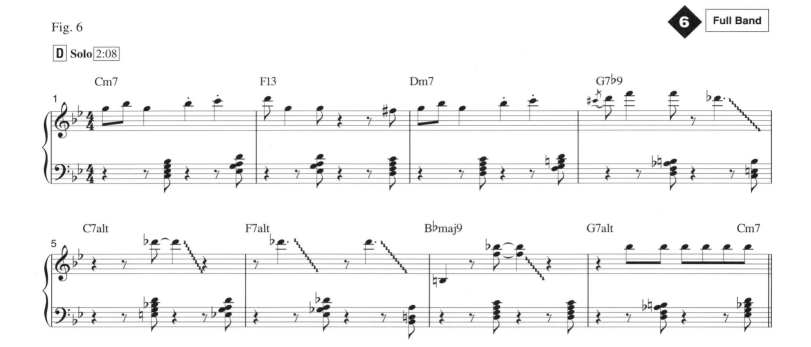

Figure 7–Ending

This is Garland-esque in the extreme—an avalanche of 13th chords outlining the descending chromatic scale of B♭.

AL HAIG
1922–1982

Al Haig was one of Charlie Parker's favorite pianists. Their numerous recordings together confirm this. In jazz, a savvy accompanist who can also hit the ground running as a soloist is a valuable asset, and Haig distinguished himself in both departments.

Born in Newark, New Jersey, Haig was arguably the best of the first crop of white pianists to assimilate the innovations of bebop. Although he appeared and recorded with many jazz notables, his career was fraught with periods of obscurity. Other Caucasian pianists (George Wallington, Joe Albany, Dodo Marmarosa) suffered a similar fate in the black-dominated bop movement and paid the rent by playing piano-bar gigs or obtaining employment outside of the music business. It is difficult to determine if the source of the problem was reversed discrimination or self-imposed exile.

Haig's cleanly executed, well-constructed solos and almost psychic comping can be heard not only on recordings with Parker, but also with Stan Getz, Coleman Hawkins, Jimmy Raney, and Chet Baker. Miles Davis's groundbreaking *Birth of the Cool* sessions include Haig on four outstanding tracks.

The solo piano recordings Haig made toward the end of his life occasionally reflect his experience as a cocktail pianist working for wages. But his trio outings as a leader are consistently interesting renderings of standards and originals by top jazz composers.

EAST OF THE SUN (AND WEST OF THE MOON)
Words and Music by Brooks Bowman

Figure 8–Intro

Haig is recording live here on a radio broadcast from the Royal Roost in New York. Playing in a quartet led by Charlie Parker, Haig lays out an adroit intro with a melodic line in D♭. Measures 1 and 2 sport a I–VI–II–V harmonic sequence, but with a surprising twist—the dip to G7♭5 on the upbeat of beat 2 in the second measure. Haig ends the intro with mostly chromatic harmony. Watch for the second-inversion (5th in the bass) voicings in measures 3 and 4 (E9 and E♭9).

8 | **Full Band**

Figure 9–Solo (First 16 Measures)

It comes as no surprise that Haig distinguishes himself in the half chorus Parker has allotted him on this ABAC evergreen. Haig was used to telling effective short stories when working as a sideman. The solo's unrestricted use of sixteenth notes gives it a double-time feel overall. The passage work is scalar, with half- and/or whole-step passing tones (measures 4, 7, and 13) and descending chromatics (measures 3, 8, and 12) serving as connecting tissue between chord tones. Exceptionally, however, measures 6 and 10 are almost pure arpeggios. Haig's frequent use of left-hand 10ths suggests that Tatum is not far from his thoughts.

Fig. 9

9 Full Band

B Solo

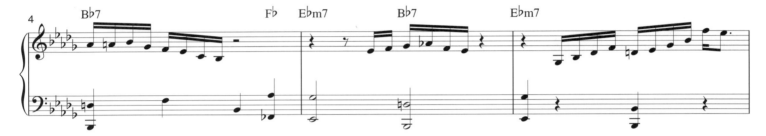

BARRY HARRIS
1929–

Harris learned his bop lessons well from Bud Powell and Thelonious Monk recordings in his native Detroit. Although he clearly owes a debt to both masters, he is far from a slavish imitator of either of their styles.

When he left the Midwest to move to New York in the 1960s, he was ready to take on the competition in a city rife with reputable, two-fisted piano players. Harris showed that his diminutive size was no indication of his musical stature and soon became a fixture on the Big Apple's jazz scene. He has recorded extensively both as a sideman and leader. A capable solo pianist, he recorded *Listen to Barry Harris*, an excellent, unaccompanied session for Riverside in 1960, when such projects were not in fashion.

Active both as a teacher and a performer, Harris's reaction to the self-conscious blues cliches that plague many young pianists is evident in a remark he once made to record producer Orrin Keepnews: "If we're going to play 'Star Eyes,' let's not play 'Star Eyes Blues'."

In recent years, Harris has beaten the debilitating effects of a stroke by undergoing exhaustive physical therapy and mustering considerable determination.

BODY AND SOUL
Words by Edward Heyman, Robert Sour and Frank Eyton
Music by John Green

Figure 10–First 16 Measures Extended to 19 Measures

Jazz players have been drawn to this 32-bar AABA song ever since Coleman Hawkins recorded it in 1939. Harris's reading of it in D♭, the original key, is a model of solo piano jazz at ballad tempo. Free of cocktail lounge excesses, but warmly convincing, it doesn't cheat lovers of sunsets and dinners by candlelight. Harris only decorates the melody at measures 4, 5, and 13. The latter two measures feature diminished chord runs (à la Tatum) on the third and fourth beats. Rich chords throw the melody into high relief, especially at V–I cadences (measures 7–8 and 16–17) as well as other crucial places. The spikey, altered F7 on the third beat of measure 15 is a Monk-ish voicing based on the F whole tone scale (F–G–A–B–D♭–E♭). The A7♭5 on the last beat of measure 17 comes courtesy of Bud Powell.

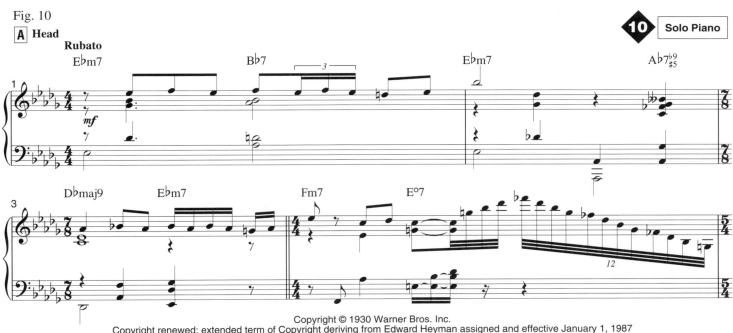

Fig. 10

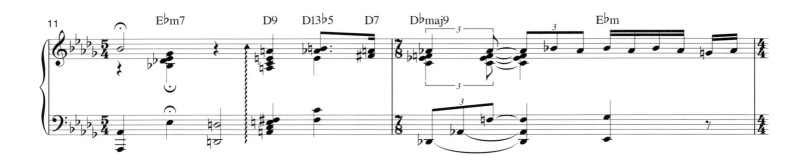

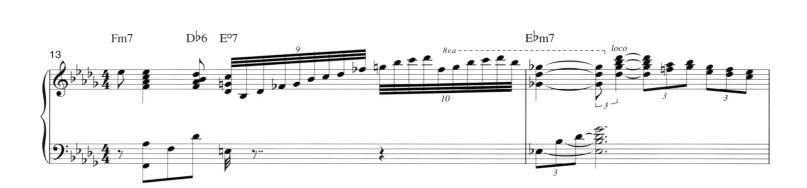

Figure 11–Head (Bridge)

In the bridge key (D), Harris tosses in a melodic tenor-voice snippet (beats 3 and 4 of measure 2) to season the C13#11 chord. Other inner voice activity concludes measure 5 and leads to a II chord (Em7) in measure 6. Harris makes his way on the slippery slope of the turnarounds in measures 8 and 9 (where most pianists are content to play the original melody's 3rds through the chromatic sequence) with clever alterings of the chords' 5ths.

Fig. 11

Figure 12–Solo (First 16 Bars)

Chord substitutions appear at measures 4 (Em7–A7 for E°7) and 7 (Am7–D7 for A♭7). An octave tremolo, a time-honored device in jazz piano tradition, is tastefully placed in measure 12. Harris's left hand exhibits a well-integrated mix of stride and bebop styles.

Fig. 12

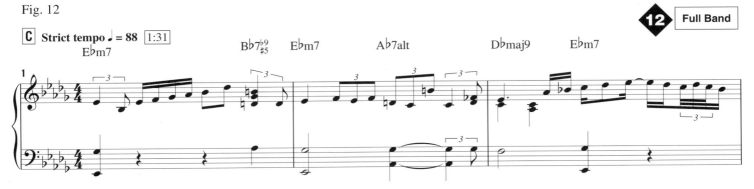

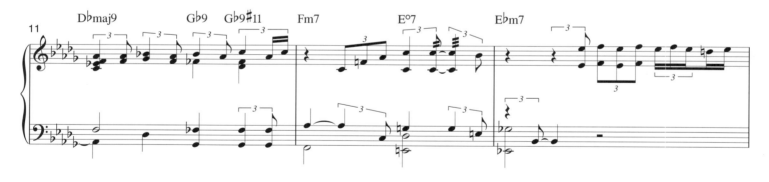

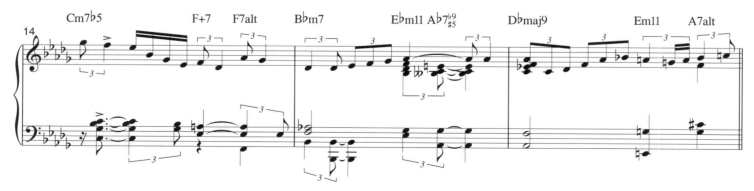

Figure 13–Solo (Bridge)

The C Mixolydian mode (C–D–E–F–G–A–B♭) is at work on the third and fourth beats of measure 2. In measure 4, Harris confirms the D chords with the root's scale members. He accents the tonic and 5th (beats 3 and 4) by preceding them with their half-step lower neighbors. Approaching the challenging turnarounds again in the last measure, Harris chooses a C7–G♭7–F7–B♭7 harmonic scheme to regain the II chord (E♭m7) of the main strain.

Fig. 13

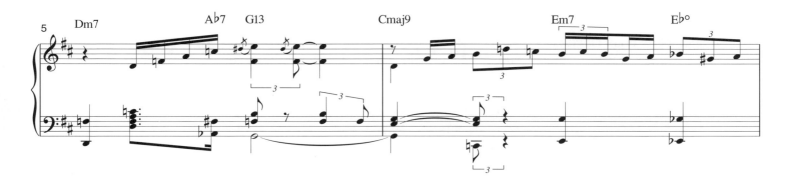

HAMPTON HAWES
1928–1977

Hampton Hawes's best playing poses an irrefutable argument against pidgeon-holing West Coast jazzmen as cooler, more restrained types than their East Coast counterparts. One must search far and wide to find harder swinging, fire-in-the-belly piano playing than Hawes at full tilt.

Born in Los Angeles, the son of a minister and a schoolteacher, Hawes began playing at the age of nine. A quick study, he was working with Big Jay McNeely and Dexter Gordon by his mid-teens. Hawes was a diamond-in-the-rough with an obvious Powell influence at this point in his career. He often said that his army years (1952–54) provided the pianos and enough isolation from the hurly-burly music scene to polish his playing and help him find his own voice.

By 1955, his recordings for Contemporary created a sensation in the jazz world. Critic Nat Hentoff, in a review for *Down Beat* magazine, was moved to write "He (Hawes) comes through here as potentially the most vital young pianist since Bud Powell in terms of fire, soul, beat, and guts."

At his peak, before his career was interrupted by a ten-year prison sentence for possession of heroin (he was pardoned by President Kennedy in 1964), Hawes had managed to reduce Powell's influence to an echo while still retaining his mentor's intensity and unbuttoned energy. The recordings he made after his re-emergence show a marked decline in style and content. He flirted with electronic instruments and sometimes crossed over into the pop market.

Raise Up Off Me, an embittered autobiography, was released shortly before Hawes died of a stroke.

I REMEMBER YOU
from the Paramount Picture *The Fleet's In*
Words by Johnny Mercer
Music by Victor Schertzinger

Figure 14–Last Solo Chorus (First 16 Measures)

In spite of its unusual construction, this song, by violinist and film director Victor Schertzinger, has become a revered standard. Schertzinger has successfully reversed the usual procedure of A (the return of the main strain) preceding C (new and terminal thematic material). The result is AABCA form. Hawes's rendition of it retains the original key of F. The pianist's unique imprint is everywhere: the clean, swinging lines punctuated by double-time outbursts of sixteenth notes; the spare left-hand work, implying chords sometimes with only single notes or tonic and seventh voicings; the phrases that tend to connect dominant to major chord sequences by half-step entry from the former to the latter. Hawes made his bones in the jazz world with performances such as this.

14 Full Band

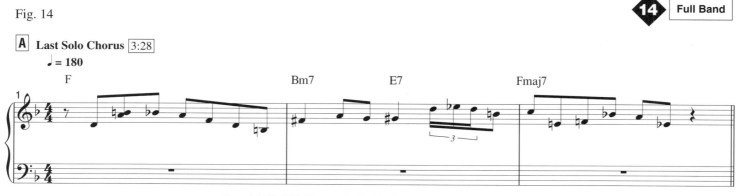

Fig. 14

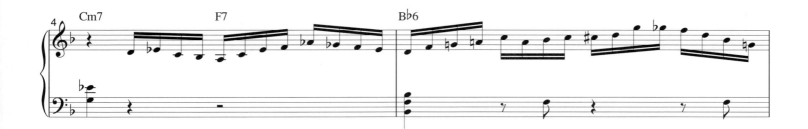

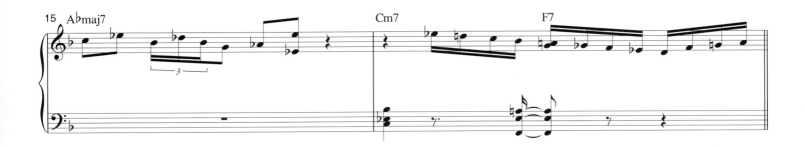

Figure 15– Solo (Bridge)

Measures 3, 4, and 5 disclose a favorite Hawes device: four-note chords reduced to two voices a 4th or 5th apart and doubled at the octave. The sound is lean but effectively funky.

Fig. 15

B Solo (Bridge) 3:49

Figure 16–Solo (Last 8 Measures)

Hawes flirts with some locked-hands voicings (close-voiced four-note chords with the top voice doubled an octave below) at measures 2 and 3, but decides to open up the chords on his way to the subdominant (B♭m7). Schertzinger's rich harmonic scheme has not tempted Hawes to play many substitutions.

Fig. 16

C Last 8 bars (Solo) 4:00

Figure 17–Ending

A tag starting on a III chord (Am7) stops short of a true modulation to A♭. The III chord returns in measure 5 followed by an A♭m9, both chords serving as a fanfare for a drum fill. Hawes takes us home in measures 7 and 8 with a V–I cadence. The sixteenth-note flourishes in the final measure are based on the F Lydian mode (F–G–A–B–C–D–E).

Fig. 17

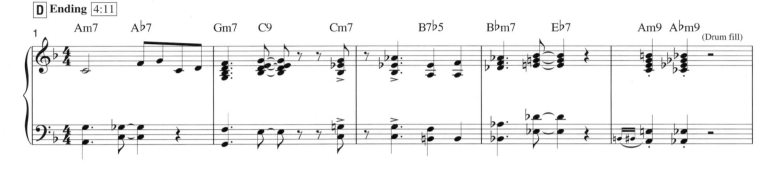

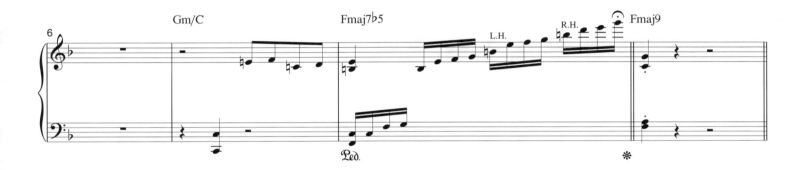

HENRY "HANK" JONES
1918–

New York's famed 52nd Street offered a plethora of talented bebop pianists in the mid-forties. Inevitably, a kind of cross-fertilization took place among the young lions as each struggled to find his own identity within the standard-bearing parameters set by Bud Powell.

Working on "the street" after an apprenticeship in his hometown of Pontiac, Michigan, Hank Jones's solution to the Powell problem was suggested by the exposure to Al Haig's playing in the tightly clustered clubs along the strip. Like Haig, Jones worked out a timeless style by fusing the older traditions of Art Tatum and Teddy Wilson with a generous sampling of the newer ideas. Other components—elegance and a sly sense of humor—were added to the mix.

Hank's career spans more than five decades of distinguished achievement as a sideman and leader. Almost every major figure in jazz has pressed him into service at one time or another, including Coleman Hawkins, Ella Fitzgerald, and Miles Davis. Fifteen years as a member of the CBS staff orchestra and a long run on Broadway as pianist/conductor in the Fats Waller hit musical *Ain't Misbehavin'* showcased the wide range of his versatility. While voluminous recordings attest to his remarkable ear and telepathic sensitivity, the piano duo recordings he made with Tommy Flanagan, John Lewis, and Marian McPartland, respectively, present those qualities in especially sharp focus.

AS LONG AS I LIVE
Lyric by Ted Koehler
Music by Harold Arlen

Figure 18–Intro

Generic intros just won't do for Hank Jones. This preamble to Harold Arlen's riffy classic in C begins on an F#13 chord, the raised 4th of the scale. The arrival of the V chord (G7♭9) in measure 3 does not proceed to the conventional V–I cadence. Instead, the last measure takes a two-chord detour before the V returns as a G13♭9. Jones, ever the fastidious harmonist, is careful to contrast the cycle of 5ths root movement of these cadential chords with a chromatic melodic line. Thad Jones, Hank's younger brother, wrote intros like this for his well-known big band charts. The true progenitor must remain a mystery.

18 Full Band

Fig. 18

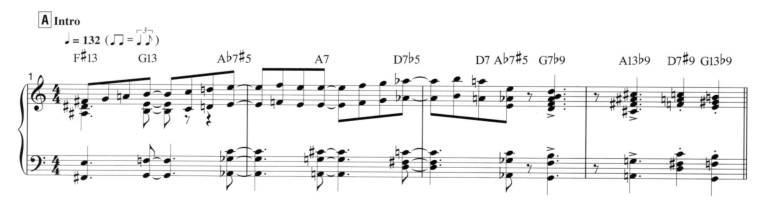

Figure 19–Head (Last 8 Measures)

Jones briefly adopts the locked-hands voicings (see the Hampton Hawes and George Shearing sections of this book) favored by many bebop pianists. After the first measure, however, his left hand breaks free from the melody and plays harmony notes in dotted quarters and eighths—a kind of Charleston rhythm. In measures 3 and 5, Jones italicizes important melody notes by using octaves. The triplets in measures 7 and 8 add a graceful momentum as the line weaves through the turnaround changes. D, the ♯11 of the A♭9♯11 chord on the first beat of measure 8, is repeated an octave lower within the triplet on the second beat.

19 Full Band

Fig. 19

Figure 20– 2nd Solo Chorus (Bridge)

    Jones's double-time passage work in this figure is typical bebop. Driven mostly by sixteenth notes, it juxtaposes arpeggiated chords (measure 1 on the fourth beat, measure 2 on the second and fourth beat, measure 3 on the third beat, measure 5 throughout) with freer scale-like components that approach the aforementioned by semitones. Triplets grace the momentum in measures 7 and 8 much as they did in Fig. 19.

Fig. 20

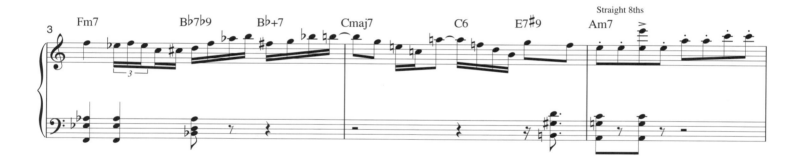

Figure 21– 2nd Solo Chorus (Last 8 Measures)

Like Al Haig, his 52nd Street colleague, Jones is inclined to fuller left-hand voicings than other pianists. Note the wide-open Eb13 on beat 4 of measure 4 whose tonic dips below the staff (a register generally reserved for unaccompanied solo playing), the five-note Ab13b5 voicing on beat 3 of measure 5, and the unabashed C6/9 chord executed in root position at the end of measure 6.

Fig. 21

THINGS AIN'T WHAT THEY USED TO BE

By Mercer Ellington

Figure 22–3rd Solo Chorus

Duke Ellington's 12-bar blues classic is played in the original key of D♭. After the riffing triplets in measure 1, Jones is diverted by the D♭ pentatonic scale (D♭–E♭–F–A♭–B♭), which has no 4th or 7th. Pentatonics also inform the subdominant (G♭7) in measure 4. The lines are lighthearted; This is not an angst-ridden blues. In measures 9, 10, and 11 we find V chords momentarily displaced by II chords. This kind of harmonic procedure is a mainstay of bebop. The turnarounds (measures 11 and 12) are bi-tonal dominant 7th chords stacked a whole step apart. Beginning on the ♭3rd step of the scale (F♭), they back-pedal toward the home key by semitones.

22 Full Band

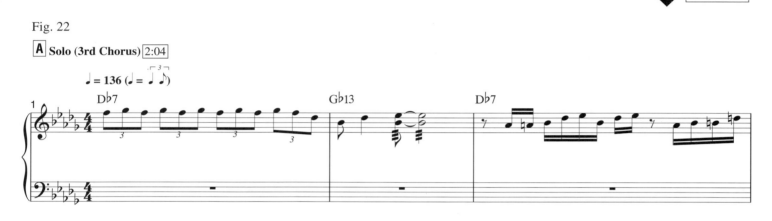

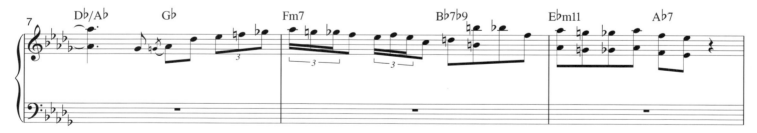

Figure 23–Solo Chorus After Bass Solo

Powell-ish sixteenth-note triplets followed by eighth notes appear on the first beat of measures 3 and 4. The execution of the seamless chain of sixteenths stretching from measures 6 to 10 is tasteful, refined, and....well, elegant. Jones ends the solo with laid-back phrases over I–VI–II–V.

Fig. 23

B Solo (6 in Chorus) 3:08

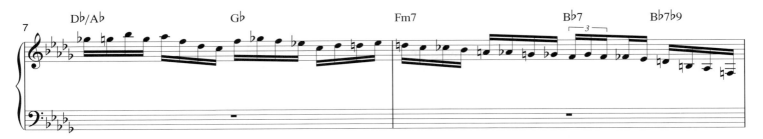

WYNTON KELLY
1931–1971

Being a fine accompanist had its drawbacks for Jamaican-born Wynton Kelly. In constant demand early in his career to provide backdrops for vocalists (most notably Dinah Washington) and prominent instrumentalists, Kelly was often forced to defer to the star power of his employers by accepting limited solo space. A handful of sessions he led on Riverside and Milestone drew some attention, but it was the recordings he made during his five-year stint (1959–63) with Miles Davis, a leader who always shared the spotlight with his sidemen, that rescued him from near oblivion.

Kelly's relaxed yet exuberant solo style was well established by the mid-sixties. With increasing opportunities to choose his own teammates for live appearances and recordings, he was often found in the congenial company of bassist Paul Chambers and drummer Jimmy Cobb. Verve released two sessions with Kelly and this outstanding rhythm section: *Undiluted* and *Smokin' at the Half Note.* The latter also featured guitarist Wes Montgomery. Other sessions followed with the pianist always swinging for the fences.

To his credit, Kelly, a compelling blues player, never stooped to the wholesale dispensing of funky licks that afflicted other pianists of the fifties and sixties. No mere parodist, Kelly was the genuine article.

ON A CLEAR DAY (YOU CAN SEE FOREVER)
from *ON A CLEAR DAY YOU CAN SEE FOREVER*
Words by Alan Jay Lerner   Music by Burton Lane

Figure 24–Head (1st 16 Measures)

Kelly revamps the melody's recurring minor 3rd interval (E down to G) in measures 1, 3, and 5. The key is F, and the first presentation is a straightforward Charleston rhythm (a dotted quarter followed by an eighth). Measure 3 calls in a B♭ Lydian mode (B♭–C–D–E–F–G–A), and measure 5 is a witty transformation that repeats the interval. Kelly's left hand comps mostly in the tenor register. Some stand-out chords include the rich, open voicing of B♭maj9 on the upbeat of 3 in measure 9 and the tight, close voicings of Gm9 and C13 in measure 15.

Fig. 24

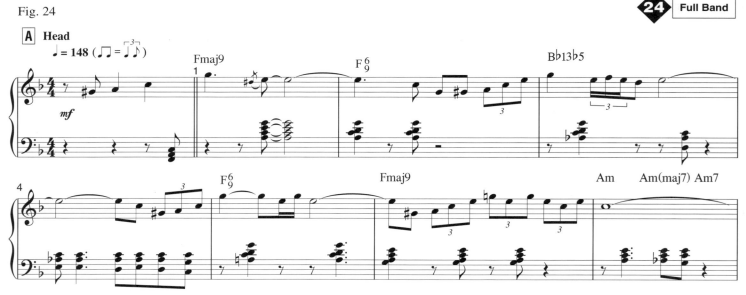

Figure 25–Head (Last Section)

Kelly is still revamping the minor 3rd interval (measure 1). This time, he conjoins it with a brief flurry of diatonic scale notes. Measures 5–10 are octave-plus-chord combinations well suited to intensify Burton Lane's climactic, if repetitive, melody. Kelly sneaks in a Charlie Parker lick over I–II–V (F–Gm7–C7) at the solo break.

Fig. 25

25 Full Band

Figure 26–Solo (First 16 Measures)

Unlike the swing players of the thirties, who were often content to build their improvisations around variations of the melody, beboppers like Kelly prefer to "blow" on the changes. The only reference to the original melody line in this figure occurs in measure 5. Kelly is mostly about the business of reckoning with the harmonic fabric. Relaxed, but with an edge (a characteristic feature of his playing), he uses semitone-filled lines and arpeggiated chords to tell his story. The E♭ diminished scale fragment (E♭–E–F♯–G–A–B♭–C–D♭) on the third and fourth beats of measure 12 colors the tale nicely.

Fig. 26

26 Full Band

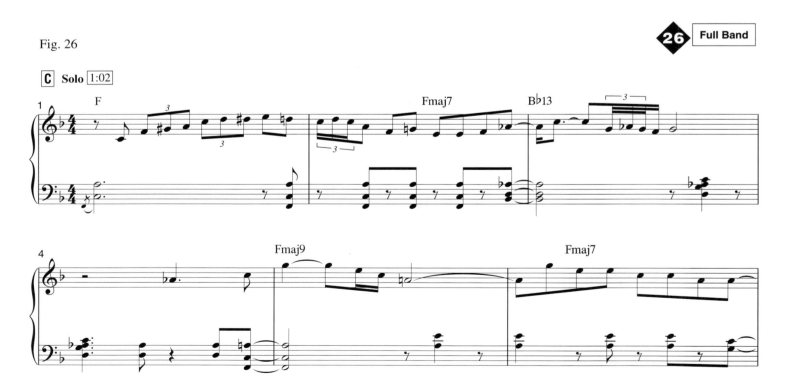

Figure 27–Solo (Bridge)

Kelly is a bluesman—witness the 3rds anticipated by grace notes, the plangent octaves, and the twangy use of 4ths and 5ths.

Fig. 27

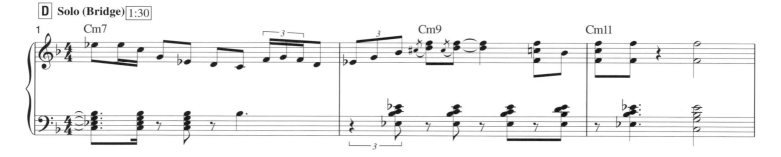

THELONIOUS MONK
1917–1982

Long before San Juan Hill, on New York's Upper West Side, became the site of Lincoln Center, Thelonious Monk was growing up there among such neighbors as James P. Johnson and Willie "The Lion" Smith. Not originally a New Yorker (he was born in Rocky Mount, North Carolina), Monk's access to those stride piano legends is manifest at times in his piano style.

The future high priest of bebop started out as a rent-party piano player and accompanist for his mother's singing in church. By the early forties, he was the house pianist at Minton's Playhouse in Harlem. There he, Charlie Parker, and Dizzy Gillespie rode the same horse toward a revolution in music.

Monk's inimitable traits are evident on his earliest recordings—an unorthodox piano technique laced with the stride style of his early mentors, the free use of dissonance, and an angular harmonic sense. His improvisations are sometimes comparable to the willy-nilly flight path of a deflated balloon.

Such a style did not readily connect with a very large audience. Indeed, success and acclaim eluded Monk until his recordings for Riverside in the late fifties. Epithets like "eccentric genius" and "a true original" began to appear in his record reviews. Crowds flocked to hear him at The Five Spot in Greenwich Village, where he sustained long and frequent engagements. His celebrity peaked on Columbia recordings in the sixties. Thereafter, his scattered history on smaller labels reflects the public's waning interest in his work.

Monk is revered as a composer. Sooner or later, every jazz musician must come to terms with "Round Midnight," "Epistrophy," "Misterioso," "Ruby, My Dear," etc.

APRIL IN PARIS
Words by E.Y. Harburg
Music by Vernon Duke

Figure 28–Head (Bridge)

Composer Alec Wilder notes in his absorbing book, *American Popular Song,* "We have heard this song so many times that it is difficult to see or hear it new." While Monk's recording of it may alienate fans of more fragrant treatments, it does not want for seeing and hearing the popular standard in fresh, new ways. Here, in the original key of C, for example, Monk resists the usual practice of bombarding the bridge with substitutions and chord extensions. He is no less effective for the spare, open voicings he chooses. Notice that few of the chord members are doubled. The C chord in measure 4 spans three octaves—without a 5th! As though to redeem himself for playing such a conventional chord, he grinds a minor 2nd (C) against the tonic of Bm11 in measure 5.

Fig. 28

28 Full Band

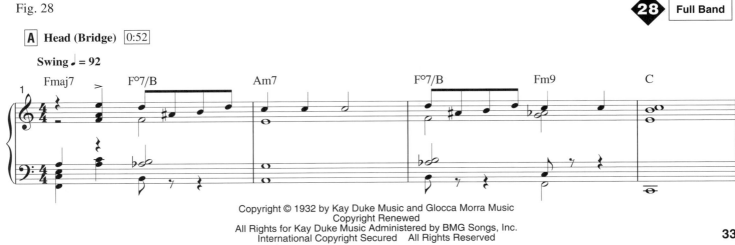

Figure 29–Head (Last 8 Measures)

More minor 2nd grinds (G against A♭) in the quarter-note triplet of measure 1. In a rare display of flash, both hands alternate in the execution of an upward run on the second, third, and fourth beats of measure 4. The usual A7 at this place is changed to A7♭5. The run makes two references to the altered 5th. Monk quickly releases the ♭9 (A♭) on the third beat of measure 6, but sustains the other members of the chord, much as he did in measure 5 of Fig. 28. The expected V chord at measure 7 never arrives—Monk uses a tritone substitution and slips into a D♭maj7–A♭7 turnaround.

Fig. 29

29 Full Band

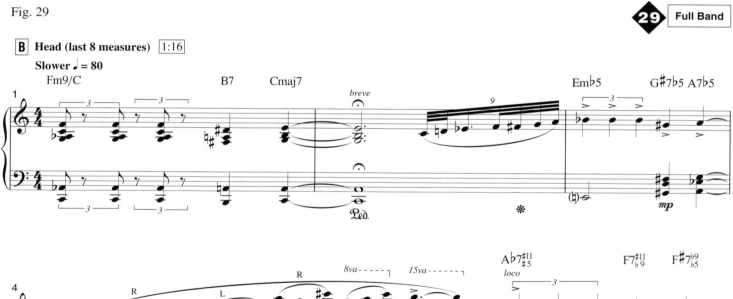

Figure 30–Solo (First 16 Measures)

Monk cheered on the innovations of the boppers without subscribing to them wholesale. He was not strictly a bebop player, as this solo section demonstrates. The jagged, staccato phrasing, the preference for larger, less scalar intervals in the line, and the often-striding left hand were anathema to the Powell school. In retrospect, Monk's ties to bebop were more philosophical than they were completely musical.

Fig. 30

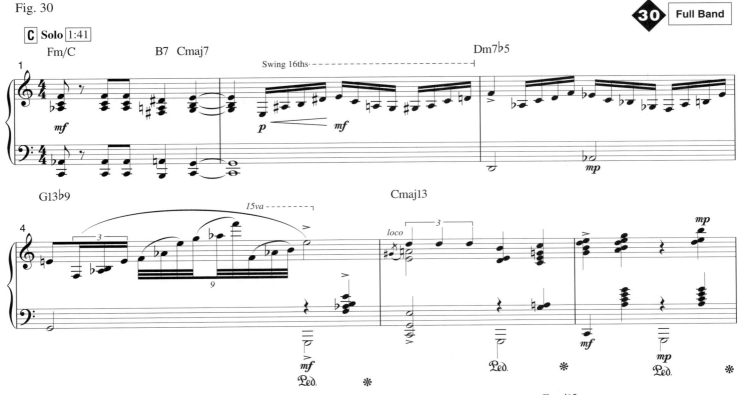

Figure 31–Solo (Bridge)

The original melody line is quoted verbatim in measures 1 and 2. It continues in measure 3, but is raised an octave—a startling effect. Measures 8 and 9 feature runs in which prominent chord members are repeated. In measure 8, the 3rd (G♯) of Emaj13 is heard four times. In measure 9, the suspended note (C) over the G7sus4 is also invoked four times.

Fig. 31

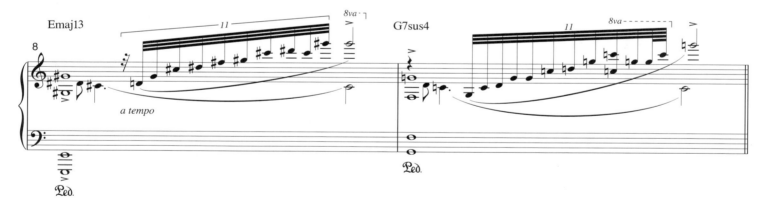

Figure 32–Reprise and Ending

Clearly, the strange but convincing final measures ending this piece on the lowered 2nd of the scale (D♭) confirm that Monk has answered the challenge implicit in Wilder's remark. He has not only found new things in the song, he has virtually recomposed it.

One more thing is worthy of note. Monk's credentials as a true virtuoso have often been questioned by the jazz community. Did he or didn't he have "chops?" Whatever your conclusion might be on the matter, Monk's execution of the fusillade of thirty-five notes in measure 5, based on the F whole tone scale (F–G–A–B–D♭–E♭), is flawless.

Fig. 32

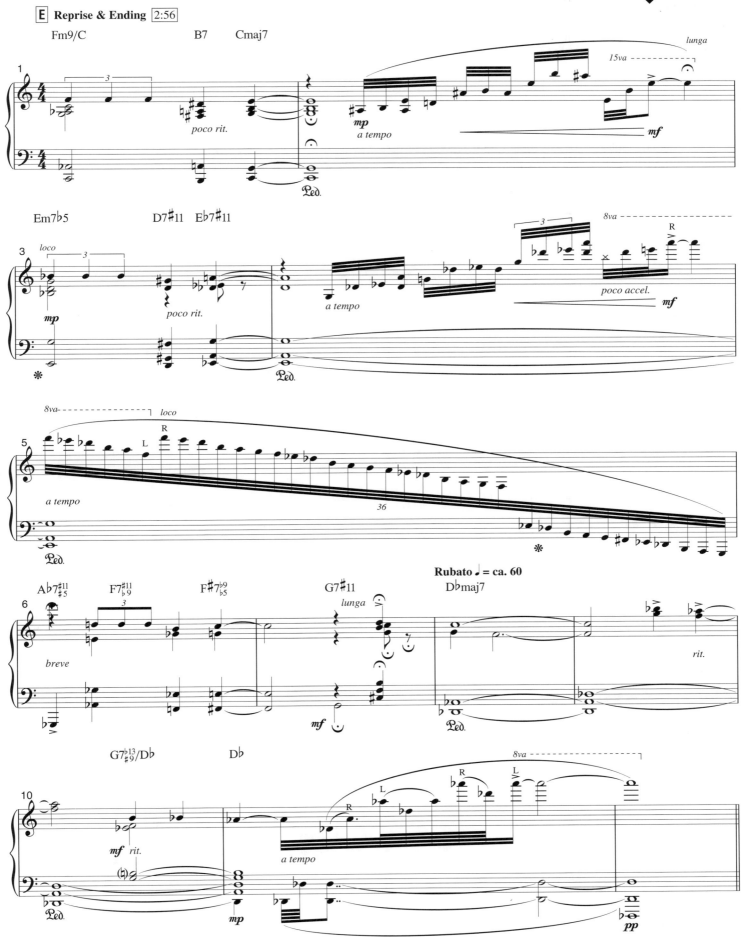

BETWEEN THE DEVIL AND THE DEEP BLUE SEA
from *RHYTHMANIA*

Lyric by Ted Koehler
Music by Harold Arlen

Figure 3– Solo (First 16 Measures)

Pianists usually sound sleep-deprived at a moderate tempo such as this, but Monk seems very much awake and vibrant. In the key of E♭ (the original key is F), the solo is a typical Monk tour de force. Sixteenth notes prevail with ties in surprising places, investing the lines with a driving, impetuous quality. Monk sometimes uses sixteenth- and eighth-note combinations where a Powell imitator would have likely played a triplet; close scrutiny of the last beats of measures 8–10 will bear this out. The pitting of craggy, lurching phrases against a stride bass in this solo is vintage Monk.

Fig. 33

33 Full Band

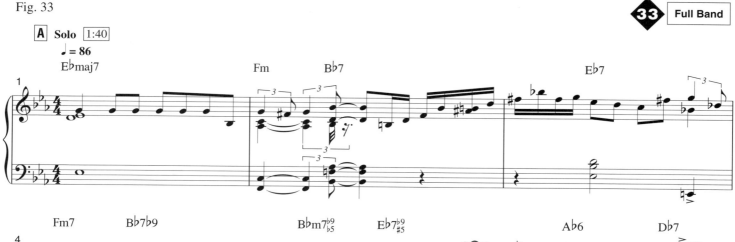

Figure 34–Solo (Bridge)

This is not Harold Arlen's bridge at all. The tonality at this point should be established on the mediant (G)—not on F7. Though Monk's memory has failed him for the ensuing eight measures, ya' gotta' love what he's come up with in their place. Measures 1–4 wrongly, but interestingly, pursue the subdominant region (A♭) with wide interval leaps in the melodic line. In measure 5, where Arlen calls for a crucial modulation to the dominant (B♭), Monk shifts to the submediant (C). This, however, permits the errant pianist to regain the home key via the cycle of 5ths.

Full Band

Fig. 34

B **Solo (Bridge)** 2:28

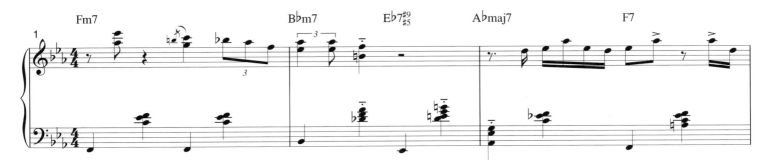

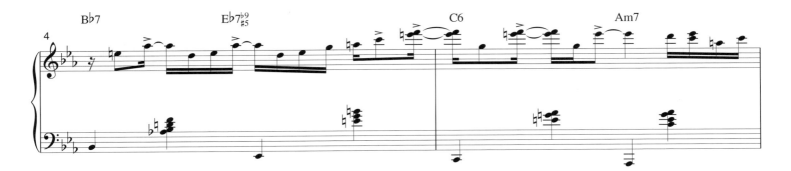

Figure 35–Solo (Last 8 Measures)

      G7 replaces the expected E♭ chord on beat 1 of the first measure, which sets the stage for a cycle of 5ths. Measures 3 and 4 observe the conventional I–VI–II–V pattern, but with some unconventional alterings—leave it to Monk to apply shock paddles to tired old chord sequences. Monk's fascination with wide interval leaps is starkly revealed by the minor 7th (F to E♭) on the third beat of measure 6.

Fig. 35

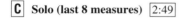

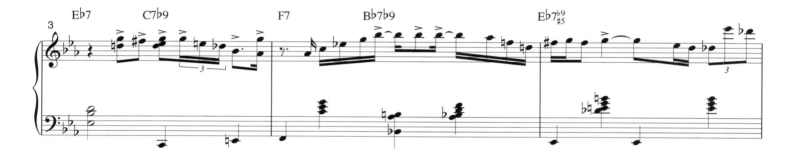

40

EARL "BUD" POWELL
1924–1966

Powell was born in NYC. The son of a stride pianist, he was classically trained from the age of five. He was barely out of his teens when he began to take part in the experimental jam sessions at Minton's Playhouse in the mid-forties. His early influences were Art Tatum and Teddy Wilson—suitable idols for a young pianist with take-no-prisoners "chops"—but the innovative company he was keeping (Monk, Parker, and Gillespie) pointed him in other directions. Soon, while working as a sideman with promising boppers like Fats Navarro, Sonny Stitt, and J.J. Johnson, his destiny as a true visionary was fulfilled.

Powell revolutionized jazz piano technique. He streamlined the oom-pah accompaniment of stride style, replacing it with spare dissonant voicings on upbeat accents. He often omitted the 3rd of the chord in his left hand and reserved it for the fleet-fingered passage work of his right. Present-day pianists have not strayed very far from his example.

Although he reached a certain amount of celebrity, Powell never enjoyed the success he so richly deserved. Paris received him well during the years he lived there (1959 to 1964), but his return to the U.S. was less than spectacular. His personal life was plagued by bouts of mental illness and substance abuse—problems which are sometimes reflected in his recordings. He died in New York City.

CHEROKEE (INDIAN LOVE SONG)
Words and Music by Ray Noble

Figure 36–Intro

Powell was a master of dramatic, heads-up intros. This one, in the key of B♭, suggests, as so many film composers have, that Native Americans are hip to pentatonics. The chords from measures 1–8 draw from the B♭ minor pentatonic scale (B♭–D♭–E♭–F–A♭). The single notes in measures 4–6 borrow the major pentatonic scale (B♭–C–D–F—G). Powell breaks all ties with literal portraiture on the last beat of measure 8 and begins to serve up the kind of intense, eighth-note-driven bebop that defined an entire generation of pianists.

Fig. 36

36 Full Band

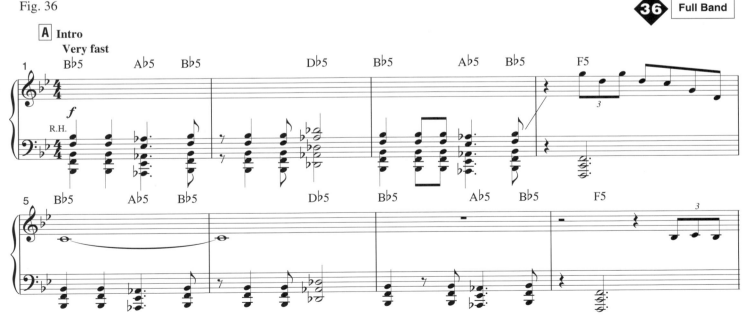

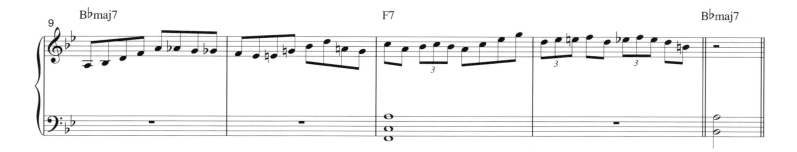

Figure 37–Reprise (First 32 Measures)

The serene flow of half and whole notes in the melody is challenged by a restless harmonic rhythm. Measures 3 and 4 contain chord changes on every beat, a procedure that is duplicated in measures 19 and 20. Even the relative tranquility of longer chord durations is threatened by chromatically active passing tones. Powell reminds us that Tatum is one of his early influences when he richly alters the C7 chord in measures 11 and 27, after the fashion of Tatum's famous recording.

Fig. 37

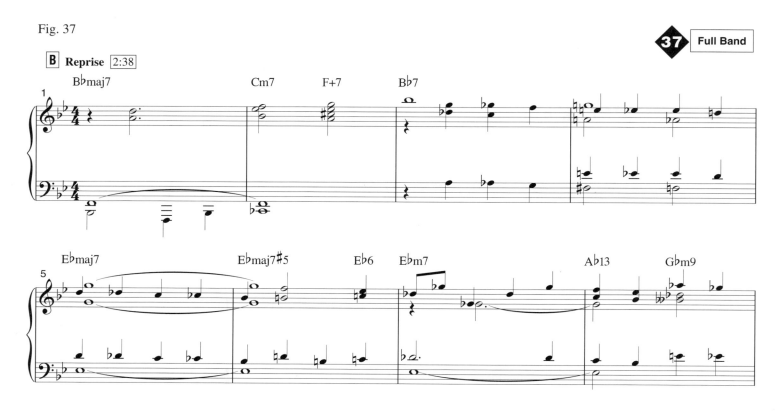

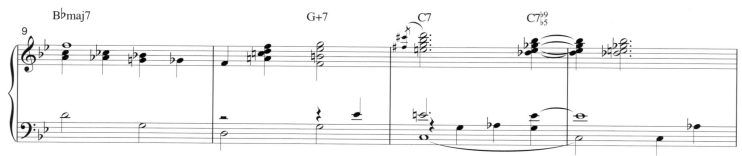

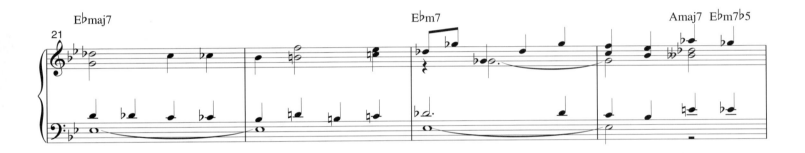

Figure 38–Reprise (Bridge)

Charlie Parker and Dizzy Gillespie liked to eliminate "lame" improvisors from the bandstand at Minton's Playhouse by calling this song for a jam tune. They knew that its slippery-slope bridge would separate the men from the boys. Powell, who frequently sat in at those sessions, was well practiced in dealing with this bridge's fast moving cycle of 5ths. Confidently, he uses a little dotted quarter- and eighth-note motif in the tenor voice to unify his ideas and contribute important notes to the chord changes. The melody borrows the motif's rhythm pattern, but expands on it by way of tied notes. At measures 7 and 8, where the tonality settles on A major after all the roiling harmonic activity, Powell keeps up the momentum with three arpeggios. The last of these alludes to the pentatonics heard in the intro.

Fig. 38

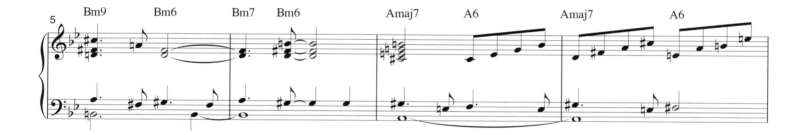

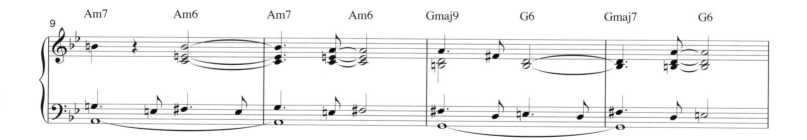

Figure 39–Reprise (Last 16 Measures) and Outro

Measures 13–16 deviate from the former statement of the main strain (Fig. 37). Powell repeats the II–♭II–I sequence he used before, but his swinging arpeggios now begin on the II chord. The ending revisits the intro with slight rhythmic modifications. In the last measure, a ♭5th (E) refuses to accept the sovereignty of the home key.

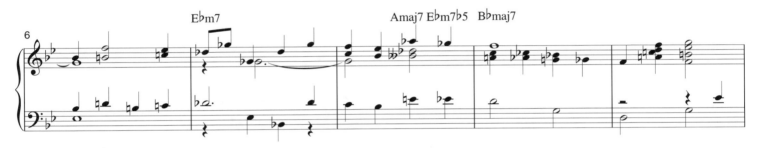

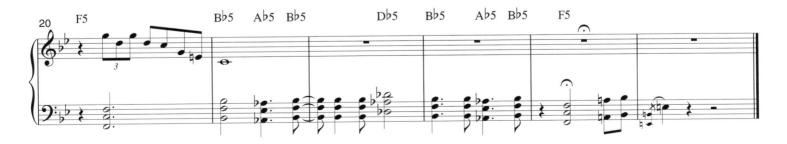

HALLUCINATIONS

By Earl "Bud" Powell

Figure 40–Head (First 16 Measures)

This Powell composition was recorded by Miles Davis's *Birth of the Cool* nonet under the title "Budo." Powell's own solo piano recording in the key of F, which we survey here, presents the piece as a little bebop humoresque—a quality that is somewhat lost in John Lewis's dramatic arrangement for Davis. The melody makes frequent use of descending chromatics and references a ♭9th and a 13th (D♭ and A, respectively) at the V chords. Powell opts for a B9♭5 in place of F7 to enter the subdominant. Two-part counterpoint (often in contrary motion, no less) alternates with thickly-voiced chords supported by octave basses to keep the texture alive and interesting.

40 Full Band

Fig. 40

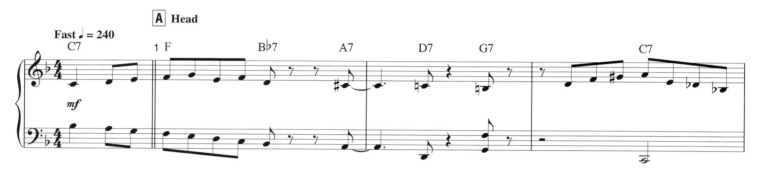

Figure 41—Head (Bridge)

This B section of the composition's AABA form is more fluid than the main strain. A swing player's articulation of these predominantly eighth-note lines would have given equal emphasis to each downbeat of the underlying quarter-note pulse. Powell, the ultimate bebopper, tends to stress the downbeats of the second and fourth quarter notes. Harmonically, Powell contrasts the II–V chords in measures 1–4 with the more step-wise bass line movement implied by the chords in measures 5–8.

Fig. 41

B Head (Bridge) 0:16

41 Full Band

Figure 42—Interlude

One of Powell's hallmarks as a composer is the addition of an interlude after the head. A thoughtfully conceived post-script, it also serves as a springboard for the solo. This one begins on the raised 4th of the scale (B) and back-pedals to the home key via II–V turnarounds. The II chords, with their ♭5ths, give added impact to the segment.

Fig. 42

C Interlude 0:32

42 Full Band

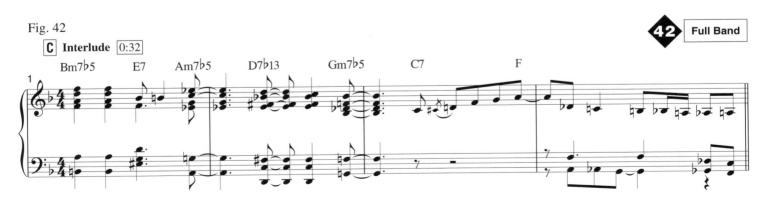

Figure 43–Solo (First 16 Measures)

Powell's once-revolutionary style is the genesis of what decades of widespread imitation have reduced to predictable common coin. It is now hard to believe that jazz piano players didn't always sound like this. After the forceful octaves in measures 1–4, Powell makes attractive arabesques out of Charlie Parker-like motifs. He rarely leaves a chord without including the defining 3rd. Cohesion is bolstered by internal rhythmic logic: i.e., the matching upbeats on the first and second beats of measures 3 and 4, the almost literal repeat of measure 11's rhythm pattern in measure 12, and the two ascending four-note figures sharing half a measure each in measure 9. Powell's innovation, the oom-pah-less left hand, stabs at upbeats with varied chord voicings, octaves, and single notes. This procedure, so controversial in years past, is now a staple of even non-jazz players.

43 Full Band

Fig. 43

D Solo 1:43

Figure 44–Solo (Bridge)

The imaginative pianist plays fast and loose with some of the original chord changes (see Fig. 41). We now have C7 in place of the Cm7 on beats 1 and 2 of measure 2. Two chords have been excised—the Am7 on beats 1 and 2 of measure 4 and the A° on beats 3 and 4 of measure 5. Powell even denounces the V chords on beats 3 and 4 of measures 6 and 8. The latter are superceded by chords founded on G♭, the lowered 2nd of the scale.

Fig. 44

Figure 45–Reprise and Ending

Powell observes the wise counsel of composer-theorist Arnold Schoenberg, "Never write a recapitulation that any copyist could write." The melody is an octave higher than it was in its first presentation. (See Fig. 40.) The harmony, shifted to the tenor register, is brighter and leaner. Measures 5–8 are repeated as a tag preceding a full cadence. A polished run (Powell was a virtuoso, after all) using the C pentatonic scale (C–D–E–G–A) concludes this object lesson on how to swing without a rhythm section.

Fig. 45

F **Reprise** 2:07

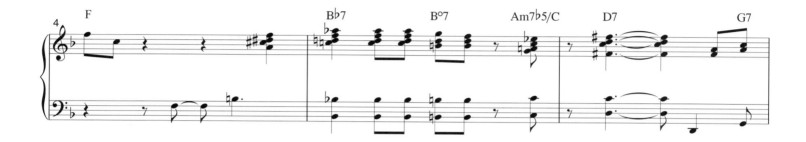

Freely

GEORGE SHEARING
1919–

Congenitally blind, George Shearing was born, the youngest of seven children, in Battersea, London. His precocious talent, revealed on the family piano, led to specialized education at the Lindin Lodge School for the Blind. He rejected several university scholarship opportunities, opting for the immediate earnings of working professionally. Soon, a career that began in neighborhood pubs expanded to recordings, engagements in top London supper clubs, and guest spots on BBC radio.

In 1947, on the advice of jazz critic Leonard Feather, Shearing crossed the Atlantic bound for New York. Founding his famous quintet in 1949, a unique blend at the time of piano, vibes, guitar, bass and drums, the now state-side leader became one of jazz's biggest attractions. The quintet's tight arrangements were based on the locked-hands style of Lionel Hampton's pianist, Milt Buckner. Its formula, easily atomized but less easily executed at fast tempos, featured the piano voiced in four-note chords. The right hand's top, or melody voice, was doubled by the left hand within an octave. The vibes played in unison with the upper melody—the guitar with the lower.

Shearing disbanded the group in 1978, appearing since then in a piano/bass duo context. Still very much in demand, the composer of the classic "Lullaby of Birdland" continues to demonstrate a sure-fingered technique, a very personal harmonic sense, and a kinder, gentler interpretation of the Powell tradition.

LULLABY OF BIRDLAND

Words by George David Weiss
Music by George Shearing

Figure 46–Intro

Shearing's blockbuster hit has undergone several stylistic incarnations over the years. This one, in the unusual key of G#minor, shows off his mastery of the Afro-Cuban idiom. The intro is an authentic montuno (a repeated, syncopated vamp) that establishes a bright tempo and a high-spirited mood. The four-measure vamp is heard four times with very subtle variations. Shearing's bass lines in measures 8 and 12 end on a G. This allows for a smooth half-step approach to the tonic of the G#minor chords that follow.

Fig. 46

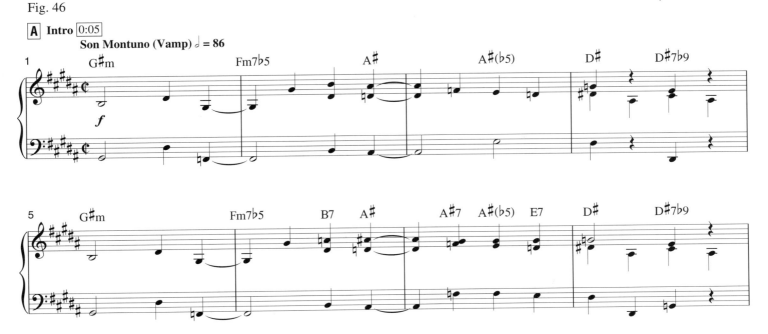

Figure 47–Head (First 16 Measures)

Buried under the theme's locked-hands treatment is the chord structure of Walter Donaldson's song "Love Me or Leave Me." The logical voice-leading of Shearing's many passing chords never violate the original genetic blueprint. Brief pauses between phrases are filled in with a few well-chosen quarter notes. The fill between measures 13 and 14 is particularly cogent. It brings about a tritone leap in the bass line (Bmaj9 to F7). A move somewhat overused by lesser beboppers, it is applied here with exquisite taste. Five-note chords, normally restricted from the four-note context of locked hands, intensify the half cadence in measures 14–16.

Fig. 47   **47** **Full Band**

B **Head** 0:15

Figure 48–Solo (Bridge)

The cosmopolitan pianist rides the changes like a true Salsero. He has rounded up the usual Latino suspects: cheery, open-voiced chords, bare octaves and/or octaves with 3rds, and II–V patterns in which the tonic of the V chord was the 11th of the II chord. The melodic line is more rhythmic than thematic. Its narrow compass rarely dips or leaps to intervals larger than a 4th. Shearing is not so Latin-ized that he has forgotten his bebop—Bud Powell might easily have played the lick in measures 9–16.

48 Full Band

Fig. 48

Figure 49–Solo (Last 16 Measures)

As if in protest to their consonant surroundings, the chords in measures 2 (beat 4) and 8 (beats 1 and 2) boldly assert themselves with the inclusion of grinding major 2nds. The relative major key of B is confirmed by several reiterations of Bmaj9 chords in measures 9 and 13. Although Powell is vaguely echoed in the melody line, Shearing is his own man harmonically when he calls upon a tritone leap in the bass line (measures 13 and 14), much as he had done in Fig. 47, to enliven the turnbacks to G# minor.

Fig. 49

HORACE SILVER
1928–

Horace's father, a Portuguese immigrant from Cape Verde, and his New England mother could never have guessed that their only child, born on Sept 2, 1928 in Waterford, Connecticut, would one day be called the Hard Bop Grandpop. As a young musician, the gospel choir Horace heard in his mother's church and the recordings of Art Tatum, Thelonious Monk, and Bud Powell were important formative influences.

He joined Stan Getz in 1950. Getz recorded one of Horace's earliest compositions, "Split Kick," a tuneful "head" over the chord changes of "There Will Never Be Another You."

From 1951 to 1956 Horace's no-nonsense, blues-soaked playing was featured in Art Blakey's quintet. He formed his own quintet in 1956 with a front line of trumpet and tenor sax. The group's repertoire was almost exclusively devoted to the leader's catchy, audience-friendly compositions and enjoyed commercial success as well as critical acclaim.

Horace's best-known compositions ("Doodlin'," "Filthy McNasty," "Sister Sadie," "Señor Blues," etc.) are either cast in blues forms or directly inspired by them. He founded the "soul jazz" movement of the late fifties and early sixties. Most of its exponents, however, were not as genuinely soulful as he was and continues to be.

THOU SWELL
from *A CONNECTICUT YANKEE*
from *WORDS AND MUSIC*
Words by Lorenz Hart
Music by Richard Rodgers

Figure 50–Head (First 16 Measures)

If ever a song was destined to be hearty fodder for bebop, that song is "Thou Swell." Amazingly, no original "heads" have been written over its obsessive II–V chords and clever use of the cycle of 5ths, but it was once one of the most over-recorded standards in the jazz repertoire, particularly in the 1950s. Silver's recording is among the most memorable. He exposes the main strain in the piano's soprano register in the key of A♭ (the original key is E♭). A swinging rhythm pattern of II–V chords, stressing the upbeat of the first beat and the downbeat of the third beat of each measure, is maintained throughout the first four measures. In measures 5–8, Silver parts company with the II–V pattern and now moves his harmony step-wise. The fill in measures 11 and 12, spanning an octave and a minor 6th, is based on Charlie Parker's habit of descending to repeat a note in an otherwise ascending arpeggio. Silver frames his turnbacks with pyramid harmony in measure 15 and edgy, altered notes in the last chord of measure 16.

◆50 Full Band

Fig. 50

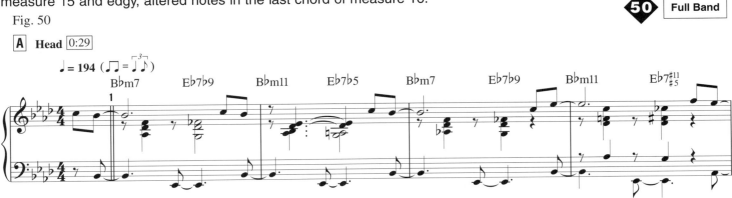

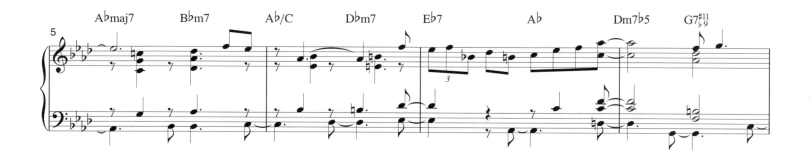

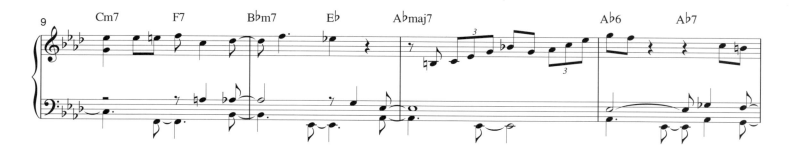

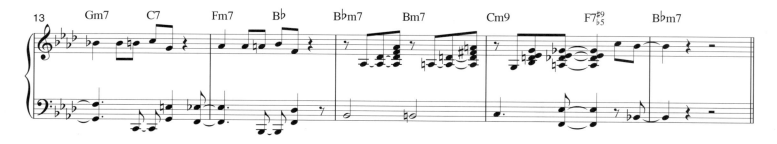

Figure 51–Head (Last 8 Measures)

The II chord (F13) in measure 4 is tantalizingly delayed. It arrives, without apology, on the second beat (not the first beat, where it is expected) and resolves the resonant voicing of a G♭13♭5. Both chords have the long-held melody note C in common. At measure 7, the arrival of a crucial chord is again delayed—the tonic (A♭) finally alights on the last beat after a zig-zag, half-step flight.

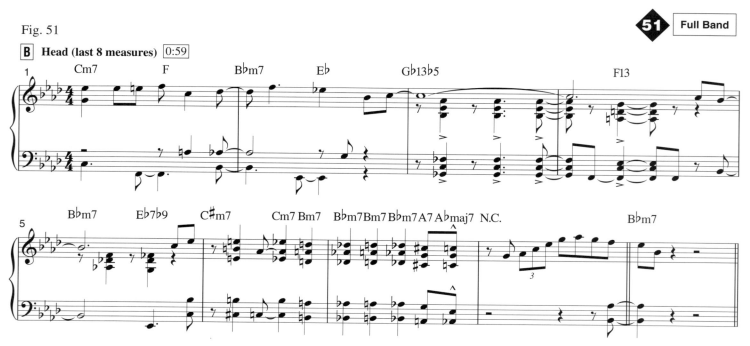

Fig. 51

B Head (last 8 measures) 0:59

51 Full Band

Figure 52–Solo (First 16 Measures)

Silver's crisp attack and scrappy phrasing are inspired by horn players. Few pianists would not be inclined to fill in the frequent "breathing" rests in this solo's right-hand lines. Fewer, still, would put the fourth beat of a measure in italics by stressing it as Silver has done in measure 6. The practice of emphasizing a weaker subdivision of common time was standard procedure for Gillespie, Parker, et al. Silver's left hand is more pianistic. It incorporates several Tatum-esque 10ths, but it is also used percussively to hammer out chords in angular tonic and 7th voicings. In measures 13, 15, and 16, it provides low and ominous support as the solo line pushes the harmonic envelope by combining an A♭ chord with a Gm7 (measure 13, beats 1 and 2), a C chord with an Fm (measure 15, beats 1 and 2), and an F chord with a B♭m7 (measure 16, beats 1 and 2).

52 **Full Band**

Fig. 52

Solo 1:09

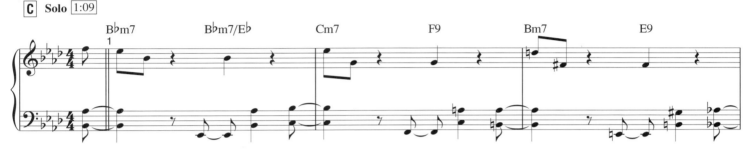

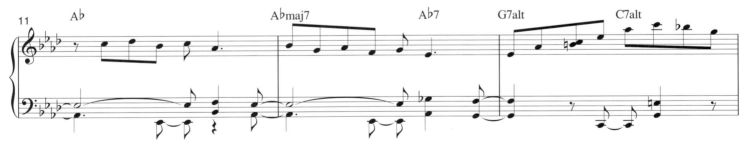

Figure 53–Solo (Last 16 Measures)

The horn-like phrases prevail and are seamlessly conjoined by well-chosen passing tones. A keen compositional instinct never allows the diversity of the ideas to disturb the logic of the whole. Even in measures 13–16 when Silver, a caustic wit when he is of a mind to be, quotes "Let It Snow, Let It Snow, Let It Snow," the illusion is that all is of one piece.

53 Full Band

Fig. 53

D Solo 1:28

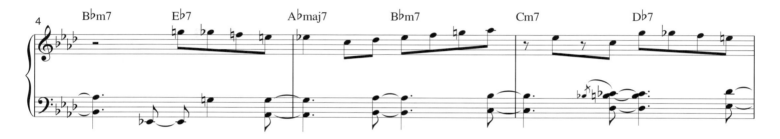

PRELUDE TO A KISS

Words by Irving Gordon and Irving Mills
Music by Duke Ellington

Figure 54–Solo (Bridge)

Silver invests "Prelude" with the appropriate emotional capital it deserves—no more, no less. The pianist rates high on the short list of certified jazz ballad players who never cross the line between sincere conviction and sophomoric bathos. The bridge is in C, the mediant of the parent key, A♭. Silver borrows the semi-tones of the melody in measure 1 to flavor the measured trill in measure 2. Steady half notes anchor the I–VI–II–V chords in the left hand throughout the figure. The right hand is freely rhapsodic. Those who feel that Silver's piano technique is unremarkable may be surprised at the virtuosity of measure 7. Silver believes in the power of simplicity and is generally loath to put on such dog and pony shows.

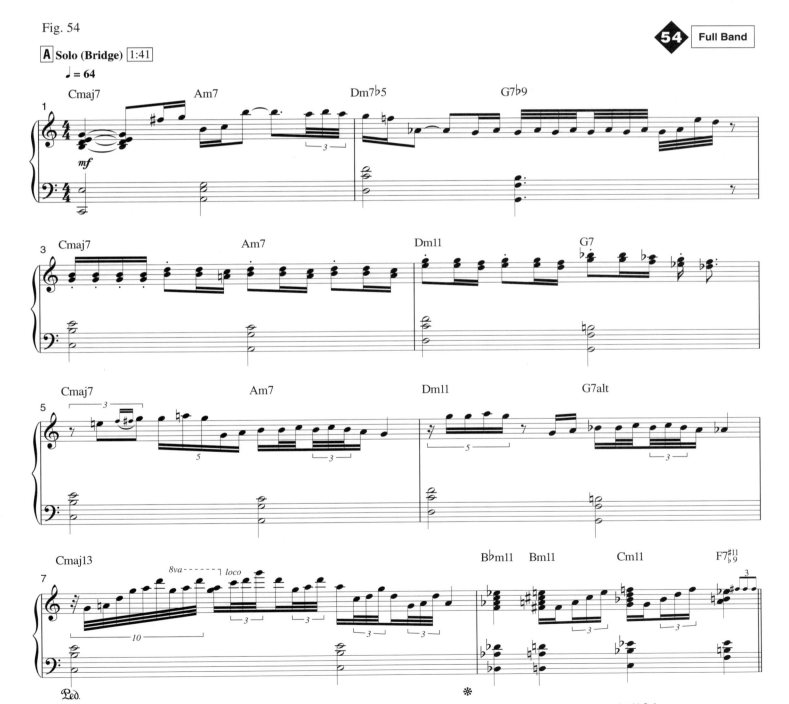

Fig. 54

Figure 55–Solo (Last 8 Measures) and Outro

Measures 3 and 4 host three replications of a swinging phrase, each of which stresses a #11th. This biting interval re-surfaces on beats 3 and 4 of measure 6, where Silver's penchant for the blues embellishes it with grace notes. Silver is momentarily distracted by locked-hands voicings in measure 7, but soon turns up the heat with a richly harmonized cycle of 5ths. The last measures are a juggernaut recall of the main strain's opening phrase.

Fig. 55

LENNIE TRISTANO
1919–1978

Blind since the ago of eleven, Chicagoan Lennie Tristano was a virtuoso pianist with a profound contempt for workaday musical values. In 1946 he moved to New York, determined to play a role in the gathering storm of bebop.

Tristano's complex, densely-voiced chords and serpentine single-note lines attracted a small but dedicated coterie of mostly white musicians, including saxophonists Warne Marsh and Lee Konitz and guitarist Billy Bauer, who eventually became his students. With a growing reputation as a musical guru, the ex-Windy City pianist opened a studio in 1950.

Tristano's few recordings are uncommonly good. Of special interest are the seven historic records he made for Capitol in 1949 with Marsh, Konitz, Bauer, and a sparkling rhythm section. On two of the tracks ("Intuition" and "Digression") the musicians were given no predetermined key, melody, chord sequence, or tempo. This practice pre-dates the "free jazz" movement of the sixties. On a later prophetic session, he dueted with himself (via overdubbing) thereby suggesting the procedure for Bill Evans's celebrated *Conversations with Myself* album.

I DON'T STAND A GHOST OF A CHANCE
Words by Bing Crosby and Ned Washington
Music by Victor Young

Figure 56–Intro and Head (First 16 Measures)

Tristano's performance of one of pop song literature's most beguiling themes is tough going for the harmonically chickenhearted. The intro's dissonant chords mask a bi-tonal scheme of C major mated with A♭ major. Only the ♭VII–I cadence in beats 3 and 4 makes the unchallenged key of C major rainwater clear. In measures 3, 4, 11, and 12, the heady parallel chords substituting the relatively tame A7♭5–Fm6 sequence of the published sheet music mirror the melody's descending half steps. Other draconian revisions of the harmony occur at beats 3 and 4 of measures 5 and 13, where Tristano moves to the sub-dominant as a minor 7th in lieu of Am. At times, the adventurous pianist traffics in clusters that hide the true identity of the chord (beat 4 of measure 8 and beat 3 of measure 10). The bi-tonality, chord clusters, and free chromaticism in Tristano's work are suggested by the practices of twentieth-century composers like Stravinsky and Bartok.

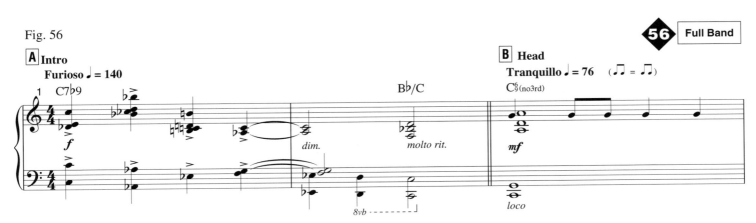

Fig. 56 / 56 Full Band

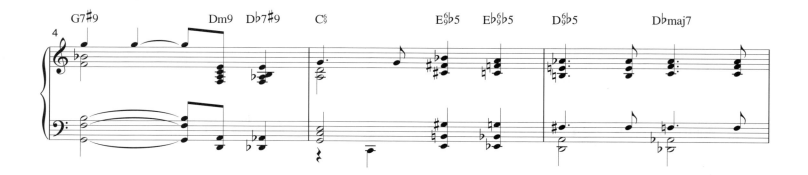

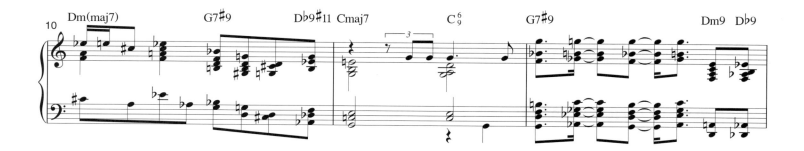

Figure 57–Bridge

Imitative counterpoint, a communicative resource all too rare in jazz playing, enriches the V chord activity in measure 2. Tristano is more linearly inclined now than he was in the main strain. His debt to Powell in the early years ("Ghost" was recorded in 1947) is more obvious here at the bridge, not only in the general stylistic approach, but particularly in measures 5 and 6. The affecting phrase therein, with its poignant use of the extensions of the chords, bears the indelible stamp of the composer of "Hallucinations." Tristano's wide interval leaps and irregular rhythms in bars 7 and 8 succeed in camouflaging a routine cycle of 5ths.

Fig. 57

C Bridge 0:53

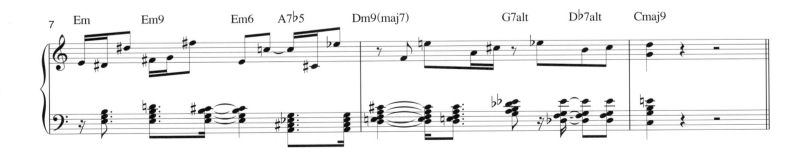

KEYBOARD *signature licks*

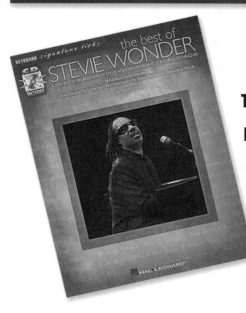

These exceptional book/CD packs teach keyboardists the techniques and styles used by popular artists from yesterday and today. Each folio breaks down the trademark riffs and licks used by these great performers.

BEST OF BEBOP PIANO
by Gene Rizzo

16 bebop piano transcriptions: April in Paris • Between the Devil and the Deep Blue Sea • I Don't Stand a Ghost of a Chance • If I Were a Bell • Lullaby of Birdland • On a Clear Day (You Can See Forever) • Satin Doll • Thou Swell • and more.
00695734 ....$19.95

BILL EVANS
by Brent Edstrom

12 songs from pianist Bill Evans, including: Five • One for Helen • The Opener • Peace Piece • Peri's Scope • Quiet Now • Re: Person I Knew • Time Remembered • Turn Out the Stars • Very Early • Waltz for Debby • 34 Skidoo.
00695714 ....$22.95

BEN FOLDS FIVE
by Todd Lowry

16 songs from four Ben Folds Five albums: Alice Childress • Battle of Who Could Care Less • Boxing • Brick • Don't Change Your Plans • Evaporated • Kate • The Last Polka • Lullabye • Magic • Narcolepsy • Philosophy • Song for the Dumped • Underground.
00695578 ....$22.95

BILLY JOEL CLASSICS: 1974-1980
by Robbie Gennet

15 popular hits from the '70s by Billy Joel: Big Shot • Captain Jack • Don't Ask Me Why • The Entertainer • Honesty • Just the Way You Are • Movin' Out (Anthony's Song) • My Life • New York State of Mind • Piano Man • Root Beer Rag • Say Goodbye to Hollywood • Scenes from an Italian Restaurant • She's Always a Woman • The Stranger.
00695581 ....$22.95

BILLY JOEL HITS: 1981-1993
by Todd Lowry

15 more hits from Billy Joel in the '80s and '90s: All About Soul • Allentown • And So It Goes • Baby Grand • I Go to Extremes • Leningrad • Lullabye (Goodnight, My Angel) • Modern Woman • Pressure • The River of Dreams • She's Got a Way • Tell Her About It • This Is the Time • Uptown Girl • You're Only Human (Second Wind).
00695582 ....$22.95

ELTON JOHN CLASSIC HITS
by Todd Lowry

10 of Elton's best are presented in this book/CD pack: Blue Eyes • Chloe • Don't Go Breaking My Heart • Don't Let the Sun Go Down on Me • Ego • I Guess That's Why They Call It the Blues • Little Jeannie • Sad Songs (Say So Much) • Someone Saved My Life Tonight • Sorry Seems to Be the Hardest Word.
00695688 ....$22.95

LENNON & McCARTNEY HITS
by Todd Lowry

Features 15 hits from A-L for keyboard by the legendary songwriting team of John Lennon and Paul McCartney. Songs include: All You Need Is Love • Back in the U.S.S.R. • The Ballad of John and Yoko • Because • Birthday • Come Together • A Day in the Life • Don't Let Me Down • Drive My Car • Get Back • Good Day Sunshine • Hello, Goodbye • Hey Jude • In My Life • Lady Madonna.
00695650 ....$22.95

LENNON & McCARTNEY FAVORITES
by Todd Lowry

16 more hits (L-Z) from this songwriting duo from The Beatles: Let It Be • The Long and Winding Road • Lucy in the Sky with Diamonds • Martha My Dear • Ob-La-Di, Ob-La-Da • Oh! Darling • Penny Lane • Revolution 9 • Rocky Raccoon • She's a Woman • Strawberry Fields Forever • We Can Work It Out • With a Little Help from My Friends • The Word • You're Going to Lose That Girl • Your Mother Should Know.
00695651 ....$22.95

BEST OF ROCK 'N' ROLL PIANO
by David Bennett Cohen

12 of the best hits for piano are presented in this pack. Songs include: At the Hop • Blueberry Hill • Brown-Eyed Handsome Man • Charlie Brown • Great Balls of Fire • Jailhouse Rock • Lucille • Rock and Roll Is Here to Stay • Runaway • Tutti Frutti • Yakety Yak • You Never Can Tell.
00695627 ....$19.95

BEST OF STEVIE WONDER
by Todd Lowry

This book/CD pack includes musical examples, lessons, biographical notes, and more for 14 of Stevie Wonder's best songs. Features: I Just Called to Say I Love You • My Cherie Amour • Part Time Lover • Sir Duke • Superstition • You Are the Sunshine of My Life • and more.
00695605 ....$22.95

Prices, contents and availability subject to change without notice.